Cosmonauts do it in Heaven

Keith Gottschalk

Published in 2021 by Hands-On Books
Cape Town, South Africa

www.modjajibooks.co.za

© Keith Gottschalk

Keith Gottschalk has asserted his right
to be identified as the author of this work.

All rights reserved.

No part of this book may be reproduced or
transmitted in any form or by any means, mechanical or
electronic, including photocopying or recording, or be
stored in any information storage or retrieval system without
permission from the publisher.

Cover photograph NASA

Book layout by Andy Thesen

Set in Legacy

ISBN: 978-1-928433-13-2

Dedicated to all who suffered ridicule, house arrest, detention, or concentration camp for their commitment to astronomy or astronautics

Consecrated to all those who sacrificed their lives for their commitment to astronomy or astronautics

FOREWORD

This collection will take you through an imaginary journey in time, from Copernicus to Einstein, the scientists who literally made space as we conceive it today. We then go through an imaginary journey through space across our solar system.

Poets have classically used the moon and stars as metaphors for romance, and such love poems are indeed here: "The Man in the Moon" and "Full Moon".

But these poems pioneer in also using space science and spaceflight terminology as metaphors for romance: "Highlights", "Argument of Perigee", "The First Refuelling in Space", "píng! pòng! Please fasten your safety belts", "One Moment", and a poem of divorce: "'*Houston we have a Problem*'".

A few poems allude to the ethical dilemmas and politics of World War II and the Cold War: "Wernher & Sergei", "The Celestial Empire", "The Titanium Monument", "Space Places", "Playing with Fire", and "Striking the Colours". A sprinkling of poems satirise South Africa's apartheid history: "First Night", "The Moon is Coming", "An Arresting Moment", "'*We demand Physics!*'", and "Report from Outer Space".

But most of all, these poems go beyond the astronaut and cosmonaut celebrities to rejoice in and celebrate the unknown astronomers, engineers, inventors, mathematicians, mechanics, scientists, and technicians who made it all possible: "Ride the Rainbow", "The Navigators", "Highlights", "First Light", "Fast Track", "New Moon", "'*Beginning of a Beginning*'", "Now to Begin", and "Square Kilometre Array". The struggle of women to win participation in astronomy, aviation, and astronautics is celebrated in "The Woman from the Krasny Perekop Textile Mill".

Enjoy reading this collection as much as audiences enjoyed seeing and hearing it performed over three decades.

Thank you to the Lansdowne Local Writers' Group (originally of the Congress of South African Writers) who has given me feedback and critique over the three decades of composing these poems.

The publication of this collection was only possible due to a generous bequest from Laurel Brodsley, who is here remembered with much appreciation.

Contents

Foreword	v
MAKING SPACE	**1**
True Confessions:	2
Street-smart canon of Frauenburg cathedral	3
The Unstarry Messenger	5
Protestant Professor of Prague	7
A Matter of some Gravity	8
Ride the Rainbow	9
The Navigators	10
Highlights	12
"*We demand Physics!*"	14
As the Sun sets	15
First Light	16
Twentieth century Physics	17
ESKOM media release	18
MAKING OUT	**21**
Prologue	22
Creation	23
The golf course on Pakachoag Road	24
The engineer from Transylvania	25
Ascension	26
Wernher & Sergei	27
The Celestial Empire	28
Chinese translation by Szu-chi Chen	29
The Titanium Monument	30
Space Places	32
Playing with Fire	34
Hyperplane & Avatar Spaceplanes	35
Expendable Launch Vehicles	36
We who are not Angels	37
GETTING HIGH	**39**
Getting High	40
Fast Track	42
New Moon	43
Joy of Flying	44
"*The Beginning of a Beginning*"	45
Now to Begin	47
Sergei Korolev House, Moscow	49
Shuttle	50

A Star of David fell from Heaven	52
Hebrew translation by Devis Iosifzon	53
The Science Teacher	56
The Woman from the Krasny Perekop Textile Mill	57
The First Refuelling in Space	59
Argument of Perigee	60
Striking the Colours	61
Stop the world – I want to get off	62
An Arresting Moment	64

PHASES OF THE MOON   65

We refuse to forget Kondratyuk	66
píng! pòng! Please fasten your safety belts	67
One Moment	68
"Houston, we have a problem"	69
The Moon is Coming	70
First Night	72
The Man in the Moon	73
Full Moon	74
Yibuyisen'inyanga! Bring home the Moon!	75
Ukubonisa Inyanga – The moon beholds the child	76

SKY BEYOND SKY   77

Flying past the sun	78
That good vibe	80
Quicksilver	81
VENERA 13	82
Waiting for the Civilised	83
Mission to planet Earth	84
The red planet	86
Mooning around	87
Spaced out	88
Way out	89
Far out	90
Chill out	91
SHGb02+14	92
Report from Outer Space	93
Square Kilometre Array	95

Index of first lines	96
Acknowledgements	99

MAKING SPACE

The theory of a city, a poem, and of the large politics of these States;
Who believes not only in our globe with its sun and moon, but in
other globes with their suns and moons ...

– Walt Whitman: *Kosmos*

True Confessions:
WHO REALLY GAVE NIC COPERNICUS THE IDEA
THAT PTOLEMY & THE CHURCH HAD GOT IT ALL WRONG

one moonful night
Copernicus's lover whispered:
"darling, the earth moved"

Street-smart canon of Frauenburg cathedral

Nicolas Copernicus 1473–1543

his maths kept coming out wrong – it was simplest to argue:
our earth revolves around the sun
when our eyes tell us – the sun revolves around the earth

– & more than our eyes told us that.

his bishop begged his canon, Copernicus: *publish.*
his cardinal cajoled his canon, Copernicus: *publish.*
but Dr Copernicus knew what was good for his health.
to contemporaries of the Inquisition
publication might just mean priority
for more than a learned journal.

so in the closet his manuscript stagnated.
the author's quill added a dedication to the pope.
without telling the author
frightened publisher added a preface
that this was only a work of fiction; but still
countdown to this book launch kept being put on: *hold.*

his equations insisted: it is simplest to argue
our earth revolves around the sun
but his throat got this dry sensation
that Occam's razor was not the only cut-throat in town.
canons know all about predestination vs free will
free will can choose: the closet – or the casket.

> Ptolemy was wrong?
> Aristarchus was right?
> our eyes & inner ear deceive?
> equations tell the truth?

dying, last sacrament, Copernicus confessed:

> *"I held back publication 36 years*
> *for thought of the scorn which I had to fear*
> *on account of the novelty & incongruity of my theory."*

discreet to the last, cathedral servant,
it was more than scorn.
481 years before Salman Rushdie's verses
this street-smart canon knew:

> *only publish when you die*
> *lest you die when you publish.*

The Unstarry Messenger

Galileo Galilei 1564–1642

it's hard to live up to being a legend
when your back aches & your sight's failing
& you only wanted to be a telescope salesman
not a martyr.

discovering spots on the sun, phases of Venus
moons orbiting Jupiter:
– measuring mountains on the moon
as low as the mountains in Italy
between university & inquisition.

1616 – NEWS COMMUNIQUE – AGENCE FRANCE PRESSE:
    VATICAN BANS EARTH FROM ORBITING AROUND THE SUN

Galileo Galilei's scope couldn't see –
the day it shattered the crystalline spheres of the heavens
will be the day Vatican politics shat all over you:
for 206 years the hard porn of Doctor Pole & Professor Pisa
rotted on the Index.

1822 – NEWSFLASH – REUTERS:
    VATICAN UNBANS EARTH FROM ORBITING AROUND THE SUN

starry-eyed messenger bearing the news:
discoverers are never ahead of their time
– the establishment is behind the times.

1992 – NEWSBITE – CNN:
    VATICAN APOLOGISES TO GALILEO

after 13 years of appeal hearings
the politburo of the Vatican central committee
pronounced that during the Inquisition's proceedings
grave violations of Catholic legality
brought canon law into disrepute
& rules:

*Galileo Galilei
is posthumously rehabilitated
from false charges of:
Copernicanism, Protestantism, Marxism, masturbation
& letting your telescope eat meat on Fridays.*

Protestant Professor of Prague

Johannes Kepler 1571–1630

when your salary isn't paid
& your mother's on a witchcraft rap
it's hard to concentrate on maths –

Kepler's first law:
an underfunded observatory travels in an ellipse
with the budget at one of the foci.

Tycho Brahe was a perfectionist to learn from
but when the Holy Roman Empire couldn't fork out
Johannes had to cast horoscopes to make ends meet –

Kepler's second law:
unpaid astronomers moonlighting as observatory cleaners
sweep out equal areas in equal times.

the motion of Mars clinched his proof:
– Copernicus was right.

his thanks?

Kepler's third law:
the square of a research project's duration without funds
is directly proportional to the cube of your overdraft.

A Matter of some Gravity

Isaac Newton 1643–1727

you had to work your way through college
but impressed your Cambridge prof
by always minting
new ideas about gravity.

you coined the concept:
a cannon-ball round as a moon
fired as fast as a sputnik
could stay up forever – by falling.

your greatest invention was a knock-out
today's observatories are its monuments:
every time astronomers look into your mirrors
they see stars.

Isaac Newton also invented the reflecting telescope.

Ride the Rainbow

Joseph von Fraunhofer 1787–1826

full moon through silk of cloud
that too-faint moonbow:
sunshine sparkling through raindrops
cascades of colour.

this Joseph found a new coat of many colours
a pot of gold at the end of every rainbow:
a cache of data.

to reach the unreachable
needs only a prism of glass
or scratches on a pane.

von Fraunhofer recorded these talkative black lines
a celestial bar code telling us readers:

your make-up?
are you blowing hot or cold?
is your blood pressure high or low?
do you feel positive?
are you coming or going?
are you still or all in a spin?
have you a magnetic personality?
– & more!

spectrums are celestial semaphore
signalling answers, flagging the facts
our galactic information superhighway.

The Navigators

John Harrison 1693–1776

Give the museum your hourglass.
Take minutes:
we second this proposal –
Harrison spends his apprenticeship marking time.
John the Journeyman of our quest for time
Master-craftsman who got all wound up
serving time for the Board of Longitude:
your best clock lost only one second per three days
– your craft stood the test of time.

Elmer Sperry 1860–1930
Hermann Anschütz-Kaempfer 1872–1931

a standing ovation
for the dance to precision,
the Gyrocompass:
ballet trio who pirouette on three axes,
spin-doctor cubed:
pilot who never loses her balance
through vermilion of fog & vertigo:
airborne Ariadne, your life-saving hands hold taut
the golden thread of an unseen horizon.

Walter Hohmann 1880–1945

in 1925 people were locked up as lunatic
for less than this.
a year before Lufthansa was born
you published *Die Erreichbarkeit der Himmelskörper.*
Walter turned the two-body problem into the to-body solution:
elegance of the ellipse
elongating along the ecliptic.
Hohmann's music of the spheres
harmonics of gravity boosting us planet by planet.

forty-eight years later
Mariner 10 was first to prove your theory,
hitch-hiking on resonances from Venus to Mercury
pioneering trajectories for future voyagers,
giving scientists
transports of delight.

Ed Belbruno 1951–

could Ed & the three-body problem
score a *pas de trois* for heavenly dancers?

1990: A muse flew up from Tanegashima
turned into chrysanthemum that circles earth & moon.
Hiten, Heaven Flyer, set free her Hagoromo
who flew solo, moon of our Moon.

while Hiten, on wings choreographed by Belbruno
spiralled wider to the fuzzy boundary of infinity:
so changing her course as migrating wild geese
she soared up to take the watch in a higher sky.

Die Erreichbarkeit der Himmelskörper: (German) *The Accessibility of Celestial Bodies*.

Tanegashima: Japan's space port.

Hiten: Japanese moon probe named after a Buddhist angel.

Hagoromo: (Japanese) sub-probe named after the cloak of an angel.

on wings choreographed by Belbruno: Belbruno calculated the trajectory that would ensure the moon's gravity would enable its ballistic capture of Hiten at the "fuzzy boundary".

Highlights

Kristian Birkeland 1867–1917
Carl Størmer 1874–1957
James van Allen 1914–2006

not just stormy, but størmier: Carl & Kristian
navigate our Earth, this *Fram*,
bow wave cleaving the solar wind,
sheets of plasma howling past
wetting all with static
in 450 kms per second gale.

ions flew (all fuses blew)
plasma pulsed apace
our Earth was first that ever burst
into magnetospace.

solar flares, magnetic storms
skew the compass, surf the sky:
twist darting tornados of current,
choreograph this celestial dance.

all particles pulse to a triple ballet –
every second: a million helical pirouettes
every two seconds: *pas-de-jeté* between hemispheres
every hour: the firebird dance around our globe.

curtains of light
belts of death:
where protons patrol westwards,
electrons ebb eastwards.

Van Allen guards our equator: two invisible rings of death

>   lethal, volted
>   one inner, one outer.
>   Tiaras crown our poles
>   two luminous rings of beauty
>   conjugate auroras:

  with these rings wed Sun & Earth

       wed Earth & Sky
       for better & for worse
       in calm & in storm
       till the Sun cease to shine,
       & the Earth cease to spin.

radio listeners say: on ELF the aurora chorus
     sounds like a flock of birds.
the Chuvash say: when the aurora is brightest
     she is giving birth.

Three hundred thousand amps ripple the sky
induce, until we feel the earth surge
climax in a hissing crackle of power
announcing the birth: a zenith dancing flames.

green red
glows, rays, arcs, spirals, coronas
kinaesthetics crowned in pink & blue

fire dancers sky dwellers magnetic friends

try to reach down to us – flung back by breakers of sky.
lustrous exiles; forever banished beyond our membrane of air,
which nurtures life too frail, too fragile
to join the joyful vacuum of magnetic dancers.

Fram: (Norwegian) *Forward*, ship of polar explorer Fridtjof Nansen.

ELF: Extremely low frequency.

Chuvash: live mostly in Siberia.

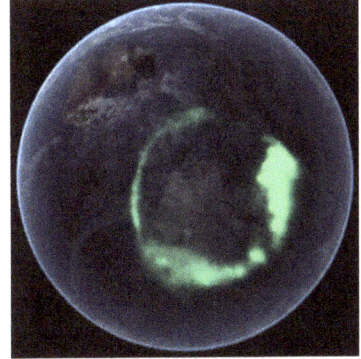

Southern Lights (photo NASA)

"We demand Physics!"

when the stars fled Cape Town
the astronomers followed
for stars hide in light
we can only see them
in the brightest dark.

we who serve the stars,
left Hartleyvale floodlights,
smog & skyglow to astrologers,
for astrology thrives on opaqueness.

starlight & irony bathe this Sutherland Karoo koppie:
a descendant of British admiralty
now precessed to this desert hill:
tonight, astronomy looks up.

Freddy Marang, night assistant,
checks spinning red dials, green screens,
keyboards his commands to electronic eye,
remembers:

"Bellville South High School
didn't teach Physics
–we demanded Physics!
eleven of us: ten boys, one girl:
so our maths teacher, Jan Persens, did the job."

in such ways the stars
help their friends win small victories
on the ground.

Freddie Marang: first black South African Night Assistant.

As the Sun sets

as the sun sets
the mourners, hoarse,
turn back from the grave.

as the sun sets
the doors close
burglar grilles are rolled down.

as the sun sets
the commuters, weary,
squeeze out of the minibus.

as the sun sets
the astronomers eat breakfast,
set off, start work.

First Light

praise poem for the Southern African Large Telescope

At the mountain's top, I reach up,
I fill my haversack with stars.
— Tatamkhulu Afrika: *Nightrider*

when the sun sets
we stand in the falling light
stretch out our arms,
catch the falling drops.

Medupe & Marang cup our CCD,
save all falling photons,
deepening into a pool of light
whose surface reflects:

stretch marks from the birth of time
hints of gravity's lenses
the pulse of stars
& mating dance of binary suns;

galaxies digitalised, heaven
captured in butterfly nets
of circuitry, red on the readout,
disked for storage: mysteries,
solved & sensuous.

Thebe Medupe: first black South African to get a doctorate in astronomy.
CCD: Charge-Coupled Device.
stretch marks from the birth of time: cosmic background radiation.

Twentieth century Physics

Heisenberg felt uncertain.
Planck went all to pieces.
Schrödinger put out a saucer of milk.
Einstein wasn't perturbed:

he knew it was all relative.

ESKOM media release

"MEGAWATT PARK was itself without megawatts yesterday when Eskom load-shedded itself. The utility could not even access its website to check which areas were without electricity as the server was down ... The Eskom head office was without power from 10am until at least 12:30pm"
— *Business Day* 11 December 2007, p2

Megawatt Park *denies* we have a power failure.
We only have a power outage.
Please note electrical engineering students *never* fail their exams; they only have exam outage.

For now, just light a match.

Eskom says it's *not* our fault. Thabo Mbeki admits it's the Government's fault. Eskom says: please be patient. Our consultants are trying to trace your missing electrons, but Werner Heisenberg is uncertain where they are hiding.

For the interim, please use your torch.

It is *not* Eskom's fault that Heisenberg suffers from severe hay fever; during pollen seasons he leaves Bavaria for the island of Heligoland.

For now, please use candles.

It is *not* Eskom's fault that
the determination of the position and momentum of a mobile electron
necessarily contains errors the product of which
cannot be less than the quantum constant h.
Eskom only learnt to read and write up to the letter g.

At this point in time, please throw another log on your braai.

Eskom says that it is all the fault of Erwin Schrödinger
that your missing electricity is both a wave & a particle. Uncle Erwin says that your missing wave has uncertainly gone out with the tide. Uncle Schrödinger says, probability is that your missing particle has fallen between the cracks.
& Eskom was just about to right-click double-click your sub-station back on when Schrödinger's cat caught & ate our computer mouse.

For the moment, please borrow from your local aquarium
ten switched-on electric eels.

It is *not* the fault of Eskom.
John Bell rang us to explain that particles at great distances
instantly transmit information to each other
to ensure that the correlation in behaviour between particles occur.
Eskom has asked Interpol to issue missing person alerts for John Bell
& your greatly distant electricity.

For now, please keep feeding nectar to one hundred fireflies in a glass jar.

Eskom: South African power utility.

MAKING OUT

SINGING my days,
Singing the great achievements of the present,
Singing the strong light works of engineers,
Our modern wonders ...
        –Walt Whitman: *Passage to India*

Each week the science club at the High School in Kaluga, where Konstantin Tsiolkovsky taught during the nineteenth century, lays a fresh bouquet of flowers on his grave in the twenty-first century (photo Keith Gottschalk). Konstantin Tsiolkovsky portrait (photo commons.wikimedia.org)

Prologue

Konstantin Tsiolkovsky 1857–1935

this aluminium aspires to heaven
this steel stretches to sky

this parabola of energy
rides the fire.

this sceptic steel
    learnt only that:

$$\Delta v = v_e \ln \frac{m_0}{m_f} = g_0 I_{sp} \ln \frac{m_0}{m_f}$$

meaning:
    the acceleration to get places
                            meaning:
        dreams of destiny
          playing with fire:
            a telescope
              a spanner
                  a welding kit.

Creation

Karel Bossart 1904-1975

	hamm-mmer
	hamm-mmer
ΔV commands:	hamm-mmer
chant:	aluminium
	niobium
	titanium.

here is no magic
only saving wealth
teaching skills
allotting work.

extrude & weld: your thinnest steel foil
　　　　　　　　into a steel balloon!
wea-ve:　　　　your finest threads
　　　　　　　　of copper & silver.
cut jewels:　　　crystals of silicon
　　　　　　　　inlaid with gold & iridium.
thought:　　　　we anoint you with thought.
memory:　　　　we curse you with memory.
bits:　　　　　　we make you smart.
drink:　　　　　cold, kelvins beyond imagining.
strength:　　　　orphan of warlords, jester of power
　　　　　　　　we grant your dream

　　　　　　　　to rise from the earth.

The Atlas and Centaur rockets were pressurised like a balloon or tyre to stand up.

Left: Robert Goddard and the first liquid propellant rocket (photo https://airandspace.si.edu/s) Right: Goddard obelisk admired by Keith Gottschalk (photo Terence Kirk)

The golf course on Pakachoag Road

Robert Goddard 1882–1945

today, your aunt's farm is a golf course
her old farmhouse now called Auburn Country Club
houses elbow right up to the fence:
the world's first liquid-fuel rocket
sure left no relics to rust.

between ice sheets on frozen fairways
walk downhill to the wooden pump-house:
only an oval flowerbed
commemorates 16 March 1926.

before it: eight hundred Chinese years of gunpowder rockets.
this hip-high obelisk marks no grave, no death.
here you, the physics prof of Clark College

demonstrated: it only happens if one makes it happen
– when you change waffle into welding no. 1

obelisk of our birth, small lift-off of our beginning.

Pakachoag hill: (native American) meaning the Hill of Pleasant Springs, was the location of the village of the Nipmuch tribe of the same name.

The engineer from Transylvania

Hermann Oberth 1894–1989

When, in 1923, you published *Die Rakete zu den Planetenräumen*
you risked that the men in white coats allocated to you
wouldn't be scientists from the laboratory.
Nor did it help your stereotype
when they discovered you live in Transylvania.

Frau in Mond got little further than the cinema screen
& a metal mock-up rocket in a Berlin department store
& one moon-struck teenager who kept hanging out
with you & the rocket.

Forty years later that teenager proved his metal:
workshopping that film into larger-than-life street theatre
scripted around your second book *Wege zur Raumschiffahrt*

plus ensuring your complementary ticket
to the VIP stand at Canaveral

for Apollo 11's Men in the Moon.

Die Rakete zu den Planetenräumen: (German) *The Rocket to Interplanetary Space.*
Frau in Mond: (German) *The Woman in the Moon,* sci-fi film.
Wege zur Raumschiffahrt: (German) *Ways to Spaceflight.*

Ascension

if you are a saint
you can ascend to heaven
on a wing & a prayer.

but as for the rest of us
we're going to need:
lots & lots

of taxpayers ...

Wernher & Sergei

Wernher von Braun 1912–1977
Sergei Korolev 1907–1966

Wernher & Sergei dream with a slide-rule
Wernher is in the SS cells at Stettin
Sergei is in the gulag at Kolyma
the dream is in hiding.

dreams subvert purposes of state
starlight is faint, too faint to shine
off coiled barbed wire; &
moonlight casts silhouettes, not votes.

this pilgrimage has stations of thorns
slaves built the royal observatory by the Liesbeeck
slaves died in the underground factory at Nordhausen
an army built the cosmodrome at Tyuratam.

sealed inside Apollo –   a valve leaked air –
   Chaffee   Dobrovolsky
   Grissom   Patsayev
   White   Volkov
burnt on the ground.   asphyxiated in heaven.

parachutes jammed –   riding on an O-ring
   Komarov   Challenger's Seven
fell from the sky.   ascended in a chariot of burning fire.

dreams draft volunteers to their cause
when astronomers look in their mirrors
they see stars
& sometimes, just occasionally
moonlight seduces the warlords.

Wernher von Braun: leader of rocketry in Germany; then in the USA.
Sergei Korolev: father of Soviet rocketry.

The Celestial Empire

Qian Xuesen 1911–2009

the Great Ocean
two shores, two realms
the western shore: jade
the eastern shore: Coca-Cola
above: the realm that calls.

on the eastern shore
you, father, birthed the rocket:
their door that clanged behind you
was not lacquered in vermilion.

on the western shore
renaissance of flying dragons:
you, midwife, let fly a new moon
you, bamboo too often battered
by madness of typhoons.

Feng Jisheng smiles with Qian Xuesen
to see the Fifth Academy, the Seventh Ministry
fly Dong Fang Hong & Shenzhou:
build from Jiuquan a silk road to the sky.

Qian Xuesen: father of Chinese spaceflight programme.
Let fly a new moon: launches China's first satellite in 1970.
Feng Jisheng: inventor of the rocket, 970 CE.
Dong Fang Hong: (Chinese) *The East is Red*, China's first satellite.
Shenzhou: (Chinese) *Divine Craft*, China's first crewed spacecraft, 1999.
Jiuquan: a Chinese space port.

神圣帝国

钱学森1911–2009

大洋
两岸两境
西岸：玉
东海岸：可口可乐
上图：调用的领域。

在东海岸
你，父亲，生了火箭：
他们在你身后叮叮当当的门
没有涂上朱红色的漆。

在西海岸
飞龙的复兴：
你，助产士，让新月飞
你，竹子经常弯曲
由于台风的疯狂。

冯继深与钱学森微笑
去看第七部第五学院
飞东方红和神舟：
从酒泉筑起一条通往天空的丝绸之路。

钱学森：中国航天计划之父。
放飞新月：1970年发射中国的第一颗卫星。
冯吉深：火箭的发明者，公元970年。
东方红：中文）东方是红色的，是中国的第一颗卫星。
神舟：中国）《神舟，中国第一架载人飞船，1999年。
酒泉：中国的太空港。

Chinese translation by Szu-Chi Chen

Faidysh-Krandievskiy's Cosmonaut memorial on Prospekt Mira, Moscow (photo Mark Wade astronautix.com)

The Titanium Monument

following Pushkin's *The Bronze Horseman*

Sergei Korolev 1907–1966

On a sun-singed steppe, Sergei stood, said:

here we shall found our cities
to cut a window through to space,
to stand on sky.

    ZVEZDNY GORODOK (Star City)

Sergei –
born in Odessa, beaten in Kolyma
zek of the First Circle, reached for the stars
thought –

from here we explore where none dared before
with guesses & guts
we train for things yet unknown
navigators & navvies
cargoes & cosmonauts
– all who will spring
through our window to the sky.

TsUP (Spaceflight Control Centre)

Korolev commanded:
Here shall rise our Admiralty.
Pilyugin – chart & navigate;
from this shore, sputniks & spacecraft
shall sail solar wind & plasma wave.

TYURATAM (Cosmodrome)

The Ministry for Exciting Machines decreed –

Engineers: let our renaissance begin!
secret Rastrellis & Zakharovs drew,
an army of workers dug; constructed
steel masts to conduct lightning down
concrete launch-pads to guide thunder up.
Quays of the cosmos, Sergei's creations, departure halls
for Mars' fields, the mountains of the moon,
the majesty of orbit:
Tyuratam, camouflaged as Baykonur,
where *Semyorka*, roaring fire,
presents a Sputnik to our planet.

---

zek: (Russian) slang for a political prisoner.
Nikolai Pilyugin: head of Soviet rocket guidance systems.
Rastrelli, Zakharov: founding architects of St. Petersburg.
Quays of the cosmos: launch pads.
Tyuratam: the Soviet Union unsuccessfully hoped to prevent NATO from locating its cosmodrome by using the name of a nearby town, Baykonur.
Semyorka: the R-7 rocket which launched Sputnik.

Space Places

its gateways reach to the sky; its flagpoles to the stars
  – Egyptian King Amenemhat II (reigned 1929–1895 BCE)

       CAPE CANAVERAL
       FLORIDA

in the Indian River, even the fish try to fly.
perhaps they leap up to salute the last Ais natives
killed or sold as slaves in 1700 Charles Town
so that in 1950 you, made by slaves in Mittelbau-Dora
could do the honours of the first lift-off,
followed by this neo-classical quest
of Atlas, Delta, Thor, Titan, Juno, Jupiter, Saturn.

today not cairns but launch pads look longingly at the sun
mooning with their memories of
when turbopumps roared & you were high
on the whiff of LOX & liquid hydrogen
while a million watched in awe,
your vibrations shaking through them,
cheering the epic man in the moon.

later, again the Banana River, transformed to mirror
reflected fire & thunder as shuttles rose, then
returned your Dear Freight to runway;
while Voyagers, Hubble, Chandra, Curiosity, so many others
revelled in your sagas of far places,
the swirl of clouds & storms,
your images from alien skies beyond dreams.

remember the African legend of the girl
who flung up embers into the sky
where they became the Milky Way?
& so you flung up these torches of titanium
tipped with aluminium, that became our space station
you, shining star who rises west, sets east
Magellan of the ninety-two minutes.

MARSHALL SPACE FLIGHT CENTER
HUNTSVILLE

when Weimar dreamers got Third Reich budgets
they could bend metal, these *Nibelungs* of an underworld,
chained to a 12-year apprenticeship to that master-craftsman of death,
before their slide-rules could again breathe free, to measure to the moon:
now their blueprints & crafts could flourish,
cut templates, weld pipes, lathe engines
to roar to the skies.

JOHNSON SPACE CENTER
HOUSTON

Houston, the eagle has landed
are the words that gave you immortality
eclipsing forever Jim Crow, oil, bling:
Houston, we have a problem
turning hubris into humility;
ever since, coaching crews, rehearsing every rescue
you prepare them for the unknowns of the void.

JET PROPULSION LABORATORY
CALIFORNIA

perched on mountainside shore of the great ocean
you fabricate fleets of robotic Odysseuses
silicon circuitry, electronic *pas de deux*
despatched to heaven, deployed to worlds, moons, rings
choreographed by your digital catechisms of ones and zeros
beaming up eternal questions, beaming back whispered echoes
from beyond the unseen, exploring our new horizons.

Ais: name of local indigenous people.

Charles Town: original name of Charleston in South Carolina.

Mittelbau-Dora: the first rocket launched from Cape Canaveral was an A4/V2 manufactured in an underground factory by concentration camp workers.

LOX: Liquid oxygen.

Dear Freight: Faroe Islands nautical slang for passengers and crew.

Nibelungs: mythical race of dwarves who live underground; highly skilled in working in precious metals.

Paul Celan: *Death Fugue*: Death is a master-craftsman from Germany.

Playing with Fire

Inter-Continental Ballistic Missiles 1957–1990

"Do you think it was right that we developed these rockets? ... We did it for spaceflight, but we needed the support of the military ... we hoped they would never be used in a war against people ... "
– Wernher von Braun, on his deathbed, 1977

Remember silos of sentinels?
titanium sentries, cold warriors of a cold war
waiting three decades for the order that never came
thirty years under the button that was never pressed.

you were an underground army that never fought,
an underground air force that never flew
you could have been mass murderers:
you whose only fight is against rust
& the budget cuts of museum directors.

Wernher & Sergei played with fire, atomic apocalypse
gambled with our lives
to get the bills paid:
gambled that you, Faust riding a microchip
would only become
our stirrup to the stars.

Hyperplane & Avatar Spaceplanes

Raghavan Gopalaswami 1936–
Abul Pakir Jamal Abdul Kalam 1931–2015
Vijay Kumar Saraswat 1951–
Puthenmadhom Venugopalan 1948–

how?

      how?

           how?

rocket engineers re-wrote, revised, ranged
with maths symbols resembling birds' feet
pecking at algorithms,
paging across sheets upon sheets
nurturing enthalpy

until finally,
with murmur of santoor, feather-light,
these equations flocked together
stretched their wings
flew off the pages

            skies
        beckoning
   India's
  into
up

Gopalaswami, Kalam, Saraswat, Venugopalan: engineers in India's Defence Research and Development Organisation who led the spaceplane project. Kalam later became President of India.

Expendable Launch Vehicles

your birth
your breaking of waters
is a flash of light
that entrances

you
anointed by light
arise from our altar
your ascent mesmerises
awesome in thunder & smoke

the Atlas moth
emerges from its cocoon
with no mouth to eat
but lives only days
to lay its eggs & pass

from birth on land
to death in the sky
your life is eight minutes
to lay an egg in orbit
that grows into a moon

son of fire
daughter of light

We who are not Angels

we who are not angels
nor born with wings
nor tithe of virtue for ascension to heaven

we had only slide rules, now software
we, who turn equation into turbopump
who craft metal to take flight

we who gave birth to the impossible
a pulse of fire soaring
a glint of light.

GETTING HIGH

O! for a muse of fire, that would ascend
The brightest heaven of invention
　　　　　　– Shakespeare: *Henry V*

Getting High

Ulli Deutschländer 1940–2013
John Moss 1943–2010

here, on every overhang & slippery stone
we confront our ancient enemy
gravity
only outwitted by strategy & muscle
& even then, only temporarily, fleetingly
while every nerve keenly aware
that the penalty for
failing
falling
breaking the laws of physics
is death.

above eight kilometres we are in the death zone:
no oxygen mask will fall from the ceiling
onto our gasping mouth;
no flight attendant can assist
for frostbite & pulmonary oedema.

Chris Bonington climbs free, joining those few
who ride the clouds, gaze down onto cloud tops;
Chuck Yeager scrambles over moraines of turbulence
juddering through the sound barrier;
Valeri Polyakov jumars up a sky full of nuts & cams
& bivouacs at 400 kms.

to strive, clinging by fingertips
to ascend, to solve an interesting problem
to ascend the next rock pitch
to turn back, to save life in foul weather;
sometimes to summit,
to ascend summit above summits
to see swirling clouds sweep & crash below
the squelch of our boots in mud, the glisten of ice & snow.

in the world of quantum physics
appearances deceive
the possibilities are uncertain
& only the impossible is true:
let your second-strongest lead
the strongest must bring up the rear, help stragglers
till we reach the ridge, crest out.

to embark on our adventure
ascenders re-packing their backpacks,
rocket engineers reviewing designs,
must pare down every kilogram:
Apollo 17 jumps free of the floodlights
abseils up a rope of fire
climbs through the night
to reach for the Moon.

Reinhold Messner soars to breath-taking summits
Bessie Colman arises on an *arête* of air to fly her colours
Liu Yang climbs to a celestial palace &
grigris down to ground.

Ulli Deutschländer, John Moss: keen South African mountain climbers who both died from cancer.

Chris Bonington: famous mountain summiteer.

Chuck Yeager: first pilot to break the sound barrier.

Valeri Polyakov: holds the record longest duration spaceflight of 437 days.

jumar: a clamp that is attached to a climbing rope.

Reinhold Messner: famous mountain summiteer.

Bessie Colman: first black woman pilot.

Liu Yang: China's first woman astronaut who visited *Tiangong* (celestial palace) space station in 2012.

grigri: an assisted braking belay device.

Fast Track

Eugen Sänger 1905–1964
Irene Bredt 1911–1983
David Urie 1932–

the visionary with a slide-rule named you: *Silbervogel*
the wind tunnel technicians joked: *bügeleisen*
but you could never iron out the funding snags,
could never fly out of that tunnel into a playful sky.

since a physics teacher
chose a book prize for that 16-year-old kid,
chose *Auf Zwei Planeten,*
three generations have taxied down this empty runway.

David said today's "the next chapter in our ride to new worlds"
he sketched on a sheet sheer geometry of power,
X-33 matched the engineer's epigram:
look good, flies good.

Eugen & Irene's flatiron
crafted from materials born after their time:
hypersonic wave-rider with engines to pole-vault horizons
you open the throttle, toss back your head.

Silbervogel laughing at gravity,
streamed delta of wings & speed, you
stand on your shock wave, surf the skies
& slide onto the silver strands of orbit.

Silbervogel: (German) silver bird.
bügeleisen: (German) flat iron.
Auf Zwei Planeten: (German) on two planets.

New Moon

4 October 1957

tre
"if we imagine" argued Newton,
"firing a cannon ball so fast

dva
that it falls per mile no more
than the Earth's own curvature

odiń
it would fall around the earth – in orbit.
that's how the moon stays up."

pusk
an aluminium beachball. outside: four car radio aerials
inside: battery, thermometer, Geiger counter

pod'yom!
Glushko's 20 engines fired Newton's cannon ball.
this was the shot that rang around the world –

100 million of us riveted to radios,
mesmerised with your frail

    beep   beep   beep

Sputnik!
awed crowds stared skywards; on the fourth evening
the world wondered at a sight never before seen:

    a new moon under a full moon.

Valentin Glushko: 1908–1989 Soviet rocket engine designer.

tre, dva, odiń, pusk, pod'yom: (Russian) three, two, one, ignition, liftoff.

Joy of Flying

trust your body – it needs to fly
your body knows what to do,
it is wind against wind
cloud over cloud
sky beyond sky ...
          – Peter Horn: *Windsurfers do it standing up*

Turbines roar, their rush surges through us
lights dim, a hush descends
mid-deck silence: only ailerons creak
as they lean into the wind, shoulder us up:
our fuselage bumps & rolls on waves of air
wings tug with winds, high-minded.

Tail-flaps rudder us, awash with direction
speeding this ocean, so insubstantial & infinite:
we praise our cities, long-surviving
we gaze down in awe on galaxies of lights
their streets recede below, the great fields too;
all shrink into pixels.

Port pulses red, starboard's green
moon's above, clouds below:
aluminium is lighter than air
as we slalom through snowscapes of sky
wings dance us past cloud-cornices, *sastrugi* of air
these *névé* of atmosphere, soaring.

Now rocketing power to leap up steps of air
ascend this stairway of sky, until horizon bends to a ball
heaven crackles indigo, & weight's only a memory
summit beyond summit, ascent above aurora
sound faster than sound, Mach 25, orbit:

Now to begin.

---

sastrugi: (Russian) wind-blown ridges of snow, hardened into ice.
névé: (Swiss French) patch of snow on rock.

"The Beginning of a Beginning"

12 April 1961

Syr Dar'ya
ancient river that flows down to the Aral
river that flows up to the sky.

Tyuratam, where Mongols racing like arrows broke camp,
Tyuratam, which for this new journey
grew Leninsk, Zvezdograd, Baykonur Cosmodrome.
Today, the kid from Gzhatsk
graduate of Luberetsky Craft School,
a foundryman's certificate,
will do work with metal what has never been done before
by man, nor woman, nor bird.

Today plants the first karagach tree
in Kazakhstan's avenue of karagach.

Poyekhali!
Yuri Alexeyevich Gagarin
cosmonaut
first person to orbit the earth;

– explorer who rocketed up 180 kms!
– test pilot who flew around the world in 89 minutes!
– foundryman who descended through the fireball!

Zarya? Kedr:
When weightlessness appears, objects swim in the cabin.
the light surface of the earth
the black sky with stars
the dividing line is thin, a film
surrounding the earth's sphere.
It's a delicate blue colour, & this transition
from the blue to the dark is gradual & lovely.
It's difficult to put it into words. Over.

12 of April 1961:
this day knows only 108 minutes
this day sees the beginning of a beginning.

"*All that you see is the beginning of a beginning*": Sergei Korolev describing Baykonur Cosmodrome to visitors.

Karagach: before lift-off, each cosmonaut plants one karagach tree.

Zarya; Kedr: radio call signs of Korolyev and Gagarin.

Now to Begin

Mir 1986–2001
International Space Station 1998–

here, no angels sing
nor winged cherubim
nor seraphim that hover over a god's throne

    here are only

        Bortinzhener Korablya
        Komandyr Korablya
        Kosmonavt Issledovatel

    here are only

        the song of antennae
        wingnuts seeking a quorum of thread
        circuits who commune with quantums

here, urging the bow on:

Leif Erikson, Zheng He,
& Phoenicians & Polynesians
whose names only the winds recall

    here, squaring the circle

        Ferdinand Magellan
        Lowell Smith
        Yuri Gagarin
            here, we cast off umbilicals

        Magellans of the 92 minutes
        construct a kite of cabins
        a flock of tetrahedrons
here, chaos of air hoses & seals

the hatching of crew
motherboards, software, templates
our learning curve is ballistic

here we calibrate

gauges, docking radar
for all who start the journey
so others may complete

here we celebrate

all who explore
where curiosity leads
now: we begin!

Left: The International Space Station (photo esa.int)
Right: Crew at the international space station (photo NASA)

Bortinzhener Korablya: (Russian) flight engineer.

Komandyr Korablya: (Russian) spacecraft commander.

Kosmonavt Issledovatel: (Russian) research cosmonaut.

Leif Erikson: Icelandic explorer of America.

Zheng He: Chinese explorer who sailed as far west as Malindi.

Ferdinand Magellan: led naval expedition to circumnavigate the world, 1519-1522.

Lowell Smith: first aerial circumnavigation of the world, 1924.

Yuri Gagarin: first cosmonaut to orbit the world, 1961.

Sergei Korolev House, Moscow

in the garden of the late rocket designer
nightingales roost in his trees

they fly to the highest branches
tilt their faces up at the sky

   & sing

      & sing

Above left: Columbia crew (photo https://airandspace.si.edu)
Above right: Challenger crew (photo NASA)
Bottom: The Challenger explosion: The space shuttle (photo cnn.com)

Shuttle

28 January 1986
1 February 2003

these are the laws of physics
immutable as those of the Medes & Persians:

you, frailness of flesh & skin
wrapped in only blueprints & hope
to plunge through furnace of plasma
burning, blasted, luminous beyond Mach-molten:
torn molecules, pink & purple,
cremating you as *sati* to the sky.

if all goes well, you shall fly
as a butterfly bolted to a bullet.
if not, your only grave shall be
Schlieren lines across a shocked sky.

to strangers,
your death shall be as beautiful as fireworks,
but to those who knew you:
grief.

they vanished
became sky:
a rain of metal tears
upon the land.

writhing,
that contrail became a cenotaph:
a wreath we laid
on our voyage to worlds.

"*Columbia was a butterfly bolted to a bullet*" – Robert Lee Hotz, *Los Angeles Times*, December 2004.

sati: (Sanskrit) custom of a Hindu widow jumping onto her husband's funeral pyre.

Schlieren: device to make shock waves visible in a wind tunnel.

A Star of David fell from Heaven

Ilan Ramon 1954–2003

Over there,
in that arched blue, on the edge of the air,
I once lived. My window was fragile.
Maybe what remained of me
were little gliders ...
    – Dan Pagis: Footprints

this lance of fire
this blowtorch of plasma
these crematoria hands of Mach 19
tore one wing off an angel:

– we fell off Jacob's ladder.

so,

Israeli astronaut Ramon's diary pages (photo flickr.com)

מָגֵן־דָּוִד נָפַל מִן הַשָּׁמַיִם

אילן רמון 1954 – 2003

"הִנֵּה שָׁם,
בַּכְּחֹל הַקָּמוּר הַהוּא, עַל שְׂפַת הָאֲוִיר,
חָיִיתִי פַּעַם. שָׁבִיר הָיָה חַלּוֹנִי.
אוּלַי שָׂרְדוּ מִמֶּנִּי
רַק דְּאָגוֹת קְטַנִּים..."
– דן פגיס: עֲקֵבוֹת [1]

חֲנִית אֵשׁ זוֹ
מַבְעֵר זֶה שֶׁל פְּלַסְמָה [2]
יְדֵי מִשְׂרָפָה אֵלּוּ שֶׁל מָאךְ 19
תָּלְשׁוּ אַחַת מִכְּנָפָיו שֶׁל מַלְאָךְ:

– נָפוֹל נָפַלְנוּ מִסַּלָּם יַעֲקֹב.

וְכָךְ:

Ramon's cloth Star of David (photo madatech.org.il)

this diary,
this cloth Star of David:
orphaned.

tell Dan Pagis it's all in our
draft agreement
on the rescue of astronauts
& the return of astronauts:

(Dear Colonel,
    we regret
        that your 17-day visa for heaven
                has expired.)

As to the yellow star: immediately
it will be torn from your chest
and will emigrate
to the sky.

As to your blue star: immediately
it will be torn from your chest
& will repatriate you
to the earth.

tumbling,
we fluttered sixty kms down
we stumbled
onto the earth
next to Palestine.

Dan Pagis: Israeli poet; amongst his poems are "Footprints" and "Draft Reparations Agreement", from which extracts are quoted here. There is an actual 1967 treaty called the Agreement on the Rescue of Astronauts, the Return of Astronauts and the Return of Objects Launched into Outer Space.

Palestine: Ilan Ramon's diary and his cloth Star of David fell to earth near a small Texas town named Palestine.

יוֹמָן זֶה,
מָגֵן־דָּוִד זֶה הָעָשׂוּי בַּד
הִתְיַתְּמוּ.

אָמְרוּ לְדָן פגיס שֶׁהַכֹּל קַיָּם
בִּטְיוּטַת הֶסְכֵּם לְשִׁלּוּמִים [3]
לְחִלּוּץ אַסְטְרוֹנָאוּטִים
וּלְהַחְזָרַת אַסְטְרוֹנָאוּטִים:

(אַלּוּף־מִשְׁנֶה נִכְבָּד,
לְצַעֲרֵנוּ
הָאַשְׁרָה שֶׁלְּךָ לִשְׁהִיָּה בַּת-17 יָמִים בַּשָּׁמַיִם
פָּג תָּקְפָּהּ.)

"*וְאֶשֶׁר לַכּוֹכָב הַצָּהֹב: מִיָּד
יִתָּלֵשׁ מֵעַל הֶחָזֶה
וְיִגַּר
לַשָּׁמַיִם.*"

אֲשֶׁר לַכּוֹכָב הַכָּחֹל: מִיָּד
יִתָּלֵשׁ מֵעַל הֶחָזֶה
וִיגֹרַשׁ אוֹתְךָ בַּחֲזָרָה
לְכַדּוּר הָאָרֶץ.

מִסְתַּחְרְרִים,
רִפְרַפְנוּ מַטָּה שִׁשִּׁים קִילוֹמֶטְרִים
מֵעָדְנוּ
עַל פְּנֵי הָאֲדָמָה
עַל יַד פָּלַסְטִין. [4]

---

[1] פגיס, דן, כל השירים: "אבא" [פרקי פרוזה] / דן פגיס, הקיבוץ המאוחד, ירושלים, 1991, ע' 141-146
[2] מושג מתחום הפיזיקה: כאשר אוויר מגיע לחום של אלפי מעלות המולקולות שבו מתפרקות והופכות לאטומים. השימו באלמנטים מעולם המדע הוא מאפיין המופיע באחדים משיריו של דן פגיס
[3] פגיס, דן, כל השירים: "אבא" [פרקי פרוזה] / דן פגיס, הקיבוץ המאוחד, ירושלים, 1991, ע' 140
[4] עיירה בשם פלסטין (Palestine) הנמצאת במזרח מדינת טקסס (Texas) שבארצות הברית שבקרבתה נמצאו השרץ המוזכרים בשיר

The Science Teacher

Christa McAuliffe 1948–1986

Classrooms produce martyrs
but never like this.

when a 587 ton test-tube cracks
class is dismissed.
when a 587 ton test-tube leaks fire
the lesson is over.

Class, NASA presents your space syllabus
to be telecast from orbit:
Lesson One: The Ultimate Field Trip.
Lesson Two: Where we've been. Where we're going. Why.

Class, preparation: wash out each test-tube
three times with distilled, de-ionized water.

when you win a competition
against 11 000 science teachers
granite & mirrors are no real memorial.

read the textbooks – thumb a pipette;
enrol as undergraduate engineer:
that's your real memorial.

your exuberance: it's fun to discover!
            it's exciting to explore!
            it's great to learn!

curiosity is our greatest challenger.

Manufactured by Morton Thiokol corporation, each space shuttle solid rocket booster, shaped like an inverted test-tube, weighed 587 tons at launch.

The Woman from the Krasny Perekop Textile Mill

Valentina Tereshkova 1937–

traditionalists always fear women who fly
the hooded finger points, pronounces the sentence:
                                                           witch
enflamed
leering eyes menace:
                                          meet your match
& the *manne* at the bar counter
grouse: just because we name you
                                        goose, chick, bird

doesn't mean you should take off, hey?

only when a suffragette flew at the king's horse
& her sisters touched down in parliament
could

        Raymonde de Laroche
                      Amelia Earhart

dance with the sky.

from Caroline Herschel to Carolyn Shoemaker
from Annie Jump Cannon to Patricia Whitelock
it was tough for angels to touch the stars.

                Valentina Tereshkova
                worked up a new tapestry
                with weft of silk of parachutes
                & the warp of skies

first
                        but the Seagull allowed to soar only once
Svetlana Savitskaya welded her colours to the mast
                                  & her voice to the Duma
Sally rode the heavens
                        lit the eternal flame remembering
Judith Resnik
                        for whose devotion the sky exacted *sati*
Mae Jemison
                        raised our colours, saluted Bessie Coleman

Helen Sharman
     commuted from a Mars factory to earth orbit
& Shannon's lucid email
    beckoning Heike Walpot
      up from her Lufthansa joystick:

"the stars are always brighter on the other side of the hatch".

Raymonde de Laroche: first woman pilot.

Amelia Earhart: first woman to fly solo across the Atlantic.

Caroline Herschel: woman astronomer, discovered several comets.

Carolyn Shoemaker: woman astronomer, discovered comet that crashed into Jupiter.

Annie Jump Cannon: woman astronomer who invented stellar classification system.

Patricia Whitelock: first woman astronomer in permanent post in South Africa.

Valentina Tereshkova: first woman cosmonaut to orbit the Earth, 16 June 1963; her radio call sign was Seagull.

Svetlana Savitskaya: second woman cosmonaut; first to weld in space.

Sally Ride: first US woman astronaut.

Judith Resnik: second US woman astronaut; died in Challenger tragedy.

Mae Jemison: first black woman astronaut.

Bessie Coleman: first black woman pilot.

Helen Sharman: first British woman astronaut.

Shannon Lucid: held the longest duration spaceflight record for a US astronaut.

Heike Walpot: Lufthansa pilot who qualified as an astronaut, but was not selected for any spaceflight.

The First Refuelling in Space

Progress 1 – Salyut 6
22 January 1978

Isaac Newton never promised it would be easy
when a male joint chases a female joint right across heaven
at 8 000 metres per second.

the small of the back is warm, fingers sometimes cold
so Soviet spacecraft come
wrapped in green thermal blanket.

soar in space
singing the sensuous longitude of the ascending node
until radio beacons wink
whisper titanium
with a murmur of thrust, spaced out:
hard docking.

electrons know every body
has its own resonance, capacity.
we internet: a circuit pulses
standing wave becomes traveling wave
delivering fuel, working fluid, breath;
the airlock opens, we offer bread & salt.

> *when we touch, our fingers*
> *feel the current: lightning bonds us.*
> *the space between your skin & mine*
> *is not a void but silent rivers;*
> *now we join ourselves*
> *with the singing threads of this new fabric:*

we couple strengths, building
for our voyage.

Argument of Perigee

It is very difficult for me to write this letter, but I have to do it. I decided that I am really not ready to get married again. At the moment I just want to be left in peace by everyone and live my life as I please, because I cannot please everyone at the same time. I just want to be able to relax and concentrate on especially my studies. It is a decision I've made which I'll have to live with, and which I will also regret at times, since I'll never find anyone like you again. But I've decided that I want to stay single & make a life for my child & me.

        Even in weightlessness, carnations bloom.
In that window-box of a greenhouse called Oasis,
bolted onto space station Mir, a most bearable
lightness of being, Russian cosmonauts hang out:
it sort of relaxes you better than aluminium & faxes.
But while the carnations bloomed they never bore seed.
No argument parted us but argument of perigee:
a precession of circumstances,
the diverging orbits of two lives;
two spaceships that passed in the night.

Space Navigation: when one body is orbiting around another body and you want to calculate where it's going to, *Argument of Perigee* is one of seven measurements you need.

Striking the Colours

7 September 1992

Commander Anatoli Solovyev
Flight Engineer Sergei Avdeyev
seal their spacesuit helmets
enter the airlock: hissing, silence, a
hatch swinging open.

Mir's first orbit soars over
the bread queue shot in the Novi Prospekt:
Zemlya i Volya! Land & Freedom!
All power to the Soviets!
& sailor Zheleznyakov:

The Constituent Assembly is closed because the guard is tired.

Mir's second orbit launches
five-year slogans:
Communism is Soviet power
plus electrification of the whole country!
– & Sputnik.

the Commander pushes out first, floating above the earth.
Sergei follows: they climb outside the hull,
reach the foot of the 14 m girder.
sudden darkness falls, climbing by torchlight
they ascend, suspended over a void.

higher than watchtowers, over the side of the earth that is night
Mir's third orbit looks down:
the archipelago of Article 58,
leaves of mammoths & *zeks*
pressed between pages of permafrost.

they reach the lanyard that shrank from their gloves.
apogee become perigee, zenith become nadir.
from this summit, 425 kms high
the last Soviet flag officially flying
strikes its colours:

The Soviet Union is closed because the guard is tired.

Article 58: Stalinist law used to sentence millions to the Gulag archipelago.
zek: (Russian) political prisoner.

Stop the world – I want to get off

Arthur C. Clarke 1917–2008

Moon circles earth every 28 days
Yuri Gagarin orbited earth in 89 minutes.
Arthur Clarke wrote for *Wireless World* way back in 1945:

   – fly high, updraft to 35 786 kms
   you'll take 24 hours to circle
   just as long as we take to circle under you
 aim your aerial only once: relay radio messages for good.

Geosynchronous orbit is:
                    hit your footprint with the ground running!
Geostationary orbit means:
                        Stop the world – I want to get off!

on this highest of perches, geostationary,
silicon wings stretch in formation
flocks of photovoltaic songbirds
sip the nectar of our sun:
turn sunshine into not vitamin D

but vocalise DC
glitter of harmonics
this chirping chorus of robotic transponders
resonates with

Handel's *Messiah*
                                      chatter of phones
LKJ
                                            faxes
Shankar's sitar
                      Horn's poetry home page on the web
Holst's *The Planets*
                            TV shows, a gossiping void
SOS Mayday Houston-we-have-a-problem
                      Adam's apples of billion-byte throats
iridescent with data.

                        Remember Syncom 3 & Tokyo 1964 Olympics?
tonight an aviary of conglomerates
                              PanAmsat 4, Skynet, BSkyB, CNN
relay the news at nine:
                             Burundi   Bosnia   Kigali   Kampuchea
this 35 000 km chasm echoes with genocides
                              embroidered as Philomela's tapestry
across an abyss of silent screams.

An Arresting Moment

Joseph Lagrange, Italian mathematician 1736–1813
Louis le Grange, South African police minister 1928–1991

two hundred years ago
his quill explored,
his equations proved:

when two massive bodies contest a space
there's five places they could trap you in;
two so stable that if you blundered upon them

you'd be locked in
suspended in the void
forever

until some violent movement got you free.
these places are named to honour Joseph: Lagrange points
four & five.
I discovered a sixth.

Challenger & I were launched into a void;
nearly the same moment;
it for seven days; I for eleven days.

Challenger travelled five million kilometres;
I, two metres.
Challenger paid tribute to Joseph Lagrange,

I, to Louis le Grange.

Lagrange points four & five: two points ahead of, and behind an orbiting planet, where all gravitational forces neutralise each other, so an object remains stationary in it.

PHASES OF THE MOON

With how sad steps, O moon, thou climb'st the skies;
How silently, and with how wan a face.
What, may it be that even in heavenly place
That busy archer his sharp arrows tries?
  – Sir Philip Sydney: *Astrophil and Stella*

We refuse to forget Kondratyuk

Yuri Kondratyuk 1897–1942

Lunar Orbit Rendezvous

ideas have ancestors
ancestors are honour
we refuse to forget Kondratyuk.
four decades before Houboult fought Wiesner
equation by equation, risk on risk;
back in 1916, when canvas biplanes creaked only one kilometre up,
you coolly proposed:

> "When spacecraft fly to moon & planets
> we'll save fuel – moor them in orbit.
> Let's launch a skiff to
> breach the surf of other skies,
> beach on new worlds; then take our leave,
> rendezvous with the mothercraft.
> Only from her orbit we return home."

Twenty-seven years after you died, fifty-three years after you wrote,
by proxy, you won the debate –
Apollo obeyed you, six times
swinging her Dear Freight around the moon,
eighteen Yankees,
safe, saving fuel, through trajectories
a Soviet scientist computed.

Dear Freight: Faroe Island nautical slang for passengers and crew.
Kondratyuk's birth name was Aleksandr Ignatiyovych Shargei.

piń! pòng!
Please fasten your safety belts &
Adjust your hormones to the upright position.
We are starting our descent to the Sea of Tranquillity

> *this parabolic love curves*
> *arching the membrane of blue flight*
> *and the deep body as our penumbral space*
> – Ingrid de Kok: *Inner Note*

let this crew
unceasingly watch where ride across the dash
those four-gauge men of the apocalypse:
temperature, pressure, voltage, vibration.

let this crew
communicate without delay their glitches:
scarred veterans of beta testing
this software is for keeps.

let this crew
make oscilloscopes dance
tune in laughter, programme for joy:
let this crew

sidestep storms of charged particles
massage trajectory so that touchdown
is not the Ocean of Storms
but the Sea of Tranquility.

One Moment

for one brief moment
a spacecraft soared
escorted the moon in her orbit

        the law of gravity decreed otherwise
        – tonight, the moon weds another sky

                gravity, immutable as Medes & Persians
                      struck down the spacecraft
                        plunged it into atmosphere

                                  burning

"Houston, we have a problem"

between moon & earth

two bodies fall through space

trapped in this broken structure

"Bus B: voltage falling"

first, amp spike –

now, falling voltage:

two bodies

deprived of purpose

dead in their coupling

plummet through a darkening space.

"Oxygen Tank 2: zero;

Oxygen Tank 1: pressure falling."

how frail is this foil sheet of sleep

as we fall through it

emptying into night.

we key:

home, home, down

to earth.

this re-joining is our parting,

with feet on the ground.

The Moon is Coming

Cape Town, 1980

THE
   MOON
      IS
         RISING

it is 0200 hours
when the moon hits the dunes by Belhar
& the dunes explode:
                  shatter amber fire:
                          bushes erupt flames.

PARAAT PARAAT PARAAT
10 AA Regiment fires tracer at the moon
the minister of justice bans all meetings
Fatti & Moni's fire all striking workers
the riot squad beats up Alexander Sinton High School pupils
armoured cars cordon off the dunes.

The Special Branch
thinks the moon is the Committee of 81.
Fattis & Monis
think the moon is the Food & Canning Workers' Union.
Generaal Magnus Malan
thinks the moon is UmKhonto we Sizwe.
The moon says: *no comment.*
The moon only speaks to the people.

AANDAG! AANDAG! AANDAG!
In their command bunker
total strategy is on the agenda.
Generaals & managing directors
posture; manipulate; threaten.

Generaal Constand Viljoen studies the map:
the workers study their pay packets.
On the map: the People's Republic of Angola.
In the pay packets: poverty
                           hunger
                           nothing!

The *Generaal* smiles
The workers don't smile
From their concrete womb
the *generaals* give birth: blitzkrieg
                             napalm
                             the armoured dash to Cela.
Out of pay packets
the workers give birth: union
                        consumer boycott
                        the strike for a living wage.

Police roadblock taxis
poke sub-machine guns under seats
but can't find the moon.
Police dogs paw the dunes
but can't track the moon.
30 Squad choppers parabats to the dunes
but can't kill the moon.
Pretoria telexes:
          – *detain Edna, Leila, Jakes.*

BUT THE MOON HAS ESCAPED

& in burnt-out buses
third-class train coaches
inside factories
chanting crescendos:

THE
   MOON
      SHALL
         RISE
            AGAIN!

Parabats: parachute troops battalion.

In 1980 Edna van Harte, Leila Patel, and Jakes Gerwel were respectively Campus Coordinator, Sociology lecturer, and Afrikaans lecturer, at the University of the Western Cape.

First Night

on my first night
I saw the moon.
Dennis Brutus only saw the stars
once in three years;
Breyten Breytenbach only saw the moon
once in seven years.

but on my first night
through the six window slits of cell C 250
through the jail yard floodlights which lash
five orange weals on the left wall
five orange weals on the right wall
the moon anoints me with silver photons.

six silver banners
on parade, half mast
slow march across the wall
signal: Strength – endure the night.

the moon
holds vigil over the captive.

Dennis Brutus, Breyten Breytenbach: poets jailed for anti-apartheid underground activities.

The Man in the Moon

seismologist selenologists
told the man in the moon:
every fourteen days
when you're closest,
when you're furthest,
deep moonquakes peak
one thousand kilometres down in the heart;
so far, so faint, they're
tremors no one can feel.

you said: it is ended. I leave.
no Eurydice followed me, only emptiness.

the man in the moon,
mooning around,
found a world without sound
with only light & dark.
here is no wind nor water,
only dust & rock.
there is no love on the symbol of love,
nor grief.
in this place there is but sky & stone
stung by meteors.

unlike Lot's wife, I could not look back:
molten salt burned within.

Full Moon

through a missing slat in the blind
a friendly moonbeam
plays across my lover's breasts

I follow its lead

Yibuyisen'inyanga! Bring home the Moon!

20 July 1969

> *shouldering my hoe, I carry home the moon*
> – Tao Ch'ien: *Five Poems* (365–427 CE)

"I believe that this nation should commit itself
to landing a moon on the taxpayer
& returning it safely to orbit:
not because it is easy but because it is hard;
because nothing will be so difficult
or expensive to accomplish;
for in whatever satellites undertake
a free moon must fully share"

Yibuyisen'inyanga!

Neil & Buzz jump off the ladder –
    That's a small step for a man
    a giant leap for mankind
we raise a flag, lower a trowel:

Yibuyisen'inyanga!

we seal treasure chests:
a ransom in pebbles & stones;
left a flag flying there
by the rockets' red glare:

   – *Yibuyisen'inyanga!*

Yibuyisen'inyanga: (isiXhosa) Bring home the moon/Diviner.
I believe ...: J.F. Kennedy speech in 1961, slightly rearranged.
Neil Armstrong & Buzz Aldrin: 20 July 1969; collect mineral samples on the moon.

Ukubonisa Inyanga – The moon beholds the child

"The awe with which [the Tembe-Thonga] people regard their surroundings is encapsulated in a haunting ritual called ukubonisa inyanga (the moon beholds the child).
      Soon after a baby is born it is taken down to the sea. A wave is allowed to wash over it before they show the child to the first full moon that rises over the ocean after its birth" – Eddie Koch

we present our machine shop
its templates & tools
its measuring & calibration
                                            – *ukubonisa inyanga*

we present our telescope
its algorithms see beyond our eyes
perceive the unknown
                                            – *ukubonisa inyanga*

we present our space station
it moves in the independence of orbit
it reigns over the sovereignty of sky
                                            –*ukubonisa inyanga*

SKY BEYOND SKY

trust your body – it needs to fly
your body knows what to do,
it is wind against wind
cloud over cloud,
sky beyond sky ...
          – Peter Horn:
            Windsurfers do it standing up

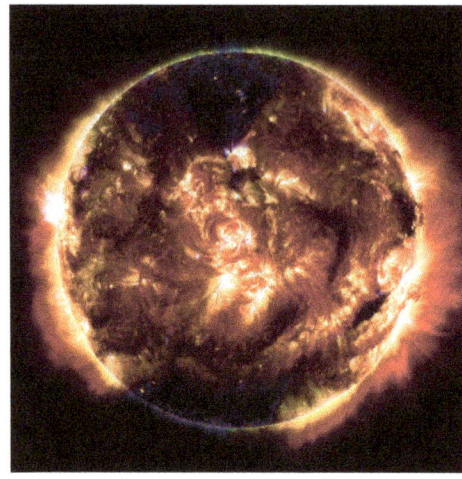

The sun
(photo NASA)

Flying past the sun

... Yearning in desire
To follow knowledge like a sinking star,
Beyond the utmost bound of human thought,
... my purpose holds.
To sail beyond the sunset ...
to strive, to seek, to find and not to yield
  – Alfred Tennyson: *Ulysses*

ESA commanded: create twins who shall seek
beyond the pillars of Hercules.
NASA miscarried. So, this sole survivor,
Ulysses, metamorphosed to robotics
we hurl at the power of Jupiter's mighty slingshot
flung upwards, to cartwheel for eternity
around the white-hot poles of the burning sun.

Roped to the mast of an orbit
forever beyond sunsets
too remote for repair
beyond all recall
where listening humans helplessly hear
your radio cries of ecstasy
at the siren singing of solar wind
at the magnetic tugs of solar plasma.

Far, too far for sighting
save by the Cyclops eyes of giant sunspots
crewed by Geiger counters clicking disapproval
of death rays darting past your hull;
this Ulysses, weatherman of the void
the ultimate watcher on the wall
warns us of flares, & solar storms.

ESA: European Space Agency. NASA lacked funding to build Ulysses' twin probe.

Jupiter's mighty slingshot: uses Jupiter's gravity to fling the spacecraft out of the solar system plane to near perpendicular.

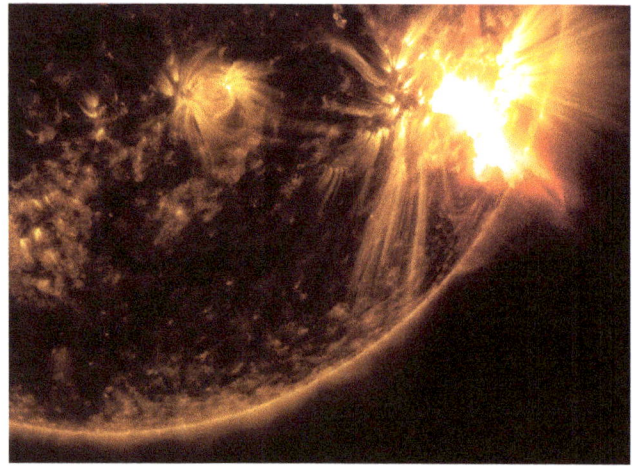

The Sun
(photo NASA)

That good vibe

that's one real good vibe
between earth & sun

it's on the down low, that vibe
point zero zero three hertz
ringing that baritone bell

a magnetic vibe saxophoning
through the solar wind, pata-pata against
our magnetosphere, stomping & shaking,
down low, so down to earth.

"Pure notes of very low-frequency sound resonate throughout the sun's interior like vibration patterns resonating in a bell. The loudest of the solar notes have frequencies clustered around 0.003 hertz, one vibration every five minutes [...] These vibrations carry out into space via the magnetic field embedded in the solar wind [...] these oscillations shake our planet very slightly by shaking earth's own magnetic field.
About a decade ago, geophysicists realised that a chorus of very faint, low-frequency hums is constantly present in the seismic records [...] the sun is inducing vibrations in our planet's magnetosphere that, in turn, literally shake the ground." – *Sky & Telescope* vol. 114, no. 6 December 2007, page 16.

Pata-pata: (isiXhosa) touch-touch – a South African dance craze of the 1950s.

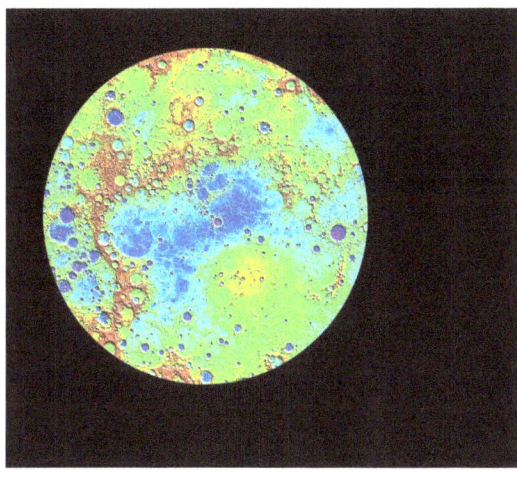

Mercury (photo NASA/ wiki commons)

Quicksilver

Mercury, fleetest of planets
always on the run from that nightmare:
the moth circling the candle flame
– go for the burn

tin melting on your equator
sweating on this treadmill, the
seventh circle of gravity, you're
no devotee of *sati* for the sun.

Venus (photo NASA/USSR)

VENERA 13

Patrick Moore 1923–2012

*If you land on Venus
you will be poisoned, fried, crushed, and corroded*
quips Patrick Moore, his
monocle gleaming like cloud cover. So
Euro myths of the goddess of love
lose out to Aztec myths of the god of war.

Compassionate Korolev
survivor of The First Circle
sent only twin robots
to the Seventh Circle
— Venera 13 & 14.

fireproofed greens
on a world without greenery:
take only photos
leave only footprints.

Patrick Moore: British populariser of astronomy.

Waiting for the Civilised

waiting for the civilised
millenarians build landing platforms on mountain tops
recalling the civilised
UFO abductees fantasise on their frequent flyer miles
phoning the civilised
Arecibo radio telescope pulses its megawatt message
to the Milky Way:

        Will you accept a reverse charge call?
but two bureaucracies
exquisite in etiquette
perfect in protocol
are ready for the civilised.

enter NASA HQ, c/o 4th & East Street, SW, DC,
    look above the foyer's Statement on Diversity
        it's nailed to the wall, prophetic in prescience:

NO ALIEN MAY PROCEED
BEYOND RECEPTION
WITHOUT AN ESCORT

& when you leave the land where
    by the rocket's red glare
        we saw the flag flying there:

IRS
ALIENS' WITHOLDING TAX:
25%

Earth (photo NASA)

Mission to planet Earth

watching Endeavour's January 1996 flight broadcast live

Pharaoh Nekau's explorers fantasised, argues Herodotus:
would you believe circumnavigators who claim
that the noonday sun lies to the watch's north?
would you buy a used galley from those Phoenicians?

Now I, a southerner,
circumnavigate a strange hemisphere
where the moon is the wrong way around
where every building has an airlock
hatched each end against the cold:
I, a stranger in a strange culture.

I, renamed temporary social security number
zero zero zero dash forty-eight dash thirty-seven-sixty-eight,
circumnavigate
strange snowscapes
where a noon sun rolls low in a *southern* sky;
this hemisphere
where silence drops from skies turned grey,
cryogenic ambush.

& when these skies blink blue
above my south-seeking face
I, mesmerised every few minutes,
witness beauty, parallel formations of
white contrails steadily threading
this blue eye of this great needle,
this hemisphere of chilled sky.

Soaring high above insistent contrails:
brought to you live by Channel 12,
Endeavour circumnavigates our globe.

Houston to Herodotus:
download it off your Explorers' home page colon backslash
Africa stop circumnavigation stop Phoenicians.

Houston, this is Mission to Planet Earth – we orbital Magellans
unreel Eratosthenes' tape measure around the world:
we endeavour to report a climate change colon.

The Cold War show has ended
its run longer than Christie's *Mousetrap*.
The patrons depart
& with them their cheque books.

Endeavour to Mission Control: we see 16 sunrises & 16 sunsets per day
we've depressurised the airlock
we walk across heaven.

Houston to Herodotus: our new circumnavigators
will practice building a space station
— tomorrow we unfold an umbilical across the sky.

Herodotus to Houston:
but at the zenith of your power
on which side stood the sun?

Pharaoh Nekau II (ruled 610–595 BCE) hired an expedition of Phoenician seamen to explore Africa's coastline and circumnavigate Africa.

Eratosthenes (276–195 BCE), the first to calculate the earth's circumference.

Mars (photo NASA/JPL/Caltech https://en.wikipedia.org/wiki/Climate_of_Mars)

The red planet

Carl Sagan 1934–1996

canals? faces? pyramids?
myths mounded upon myths to match
your polar dry icecaps
your dumped debris from cataclysmic floods.

Carl found facts more fun than fictions:
a mountain twenty-seven kilometres high
canyons, chasms, & clouds
globe-shrouding sandstorms
& two baby moons.

Venus' clouds – a runway greenhouse
Mars' dust – a nuclear winter:
myths vanishing in its morning mists
red planet of so many dreams.

Jupiter (photo NASA), Jupiter's moon Io (photo NASA)

Mooning around

Linda Morabito 1953–
Larry Soderblom 1944–

there is no such thing as a boring Galilean satellite
mused Larry, even before the news erupted.

here rules a realm with gravity & resonance
far beyond its bands, belt, Great Red Spot
        here Jupiter –
miniature solar system of seventy-nine moons
Callisto, cratered
Europa, with pack-ice crust & hidden ocean
Ganymede, mightiest of moons
Io, its flux tube the mother of all power lines
arcing its aurora into Jupiter

Io, where, navigating the pixels, Linda's eyes
first saw volcanoes on another world.

Painting of Saturn as seen from Mimas (photo Chesley Bonestell LLC)

Spaced out

Chesley Bonestell 1888–1986
Gerard Kuiper 1905–1973

rings upon rings
swirling symphonies
of skyscapes & spacescapes
    golden gates
panoramas worthy of a Bonestell
  – Saturn

grandeur of entourage
processional of sixty-two moons
for sixty-two sects to worship or calendar by:
moons Pandora & Prometheus that shepherd a ring
moons Janus & Epimetheus that swop orbits
the Titan of moons

& a braided ring
that plaits & unplaits itself
to tease mathematicians.

Chesley Bonestell: architectural renderer, illustrator, and astronomical artist who, during the 1940s and 1950s, painted scenes as they would appear from the surface of planets and moons.

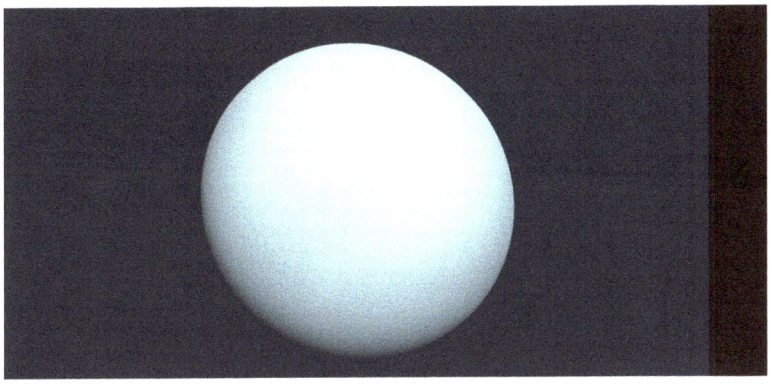
Uranus (photo NASA)

Way out

William Herschel 1738–1822
David Morrison 1940–

lotsa crooners consume da moon 'n stars
but only one musician produced a planet
– Herschel, royal organist & composer
telescoped two careers into one life

     – Uranus
perhaps bowled over by some primordial collision
with south pole slightly above north pole
a planet for all seasons

     Miranda –
moon of complexity & chevrons
rift valley of ice, horsts & grabens
scarps higher than Everest.

Neptune (photo NASA)

Far out

Johann Galle 1812–1910
Dale P Cruikshank 1939–

bluest of planets
swiftest of jet streams
high shadowed clouds
– Neptune

north pole
south pole

quadrupoles
quadrupoles   quadrupoles
quadrupoles

Triton: how our poets love
this pink & blue moon
methane frost
nitrogen geysers gushing eight kilometre plumes

Moon that orbits the wrong way around

Johann Galle: first astronomer to observe planet Neptune and know what it was.

Dale P. Cruikshank: astronomer specialising in spectroscopy of moons of Neptune, Pluto, Pluto itself, and other moons.

Pluto (photo NASA)

Chill out

Clyde Tombaugh 1906–1997
James Christy 1938–

in the year that Holst composed *The Planets*
Clyde discovered it needed one more movement

Pluto

& now Charon, Nix, Styx, Hydra, Cerberus

the style-setters for coolth

-222°C

cold beyond cold
cryogenic worlds
where air becomes ice
where ice is as hard as rock
gatekeepers to the comets & stars
ferrymen of our furthest frontier

In 2006, after this poem was composed, the International Astronomical Union voted to reclassify Pluto as a dwarf planet.

SHGb02+14

"A radio signal designated SHGb02+14 seems to be coming from a point between the constellations Pisces and Aries, where there is no obvious star or planetary system within 1000 light years. And the transmission is very weak. It has a frequency of about 1 420 megahertz (one of the main frequencies of hydrogen ..."
– New Scientist.com news 1 September 2004

"Thank you for your patience.
Your radio call is important to our stellar cluster.
All our consultants are busy.
Our network is down.
Press star & wait another millennium
or press hash & a genetically modified
cyano-nano-bacteria will attend to your call."

Andromeda Galaxy (photo Adam Evans, wikimedia.org)

Report from Outer Space

On Andromeda Galaxy
the Federation of Astronomers
convened a symposium:
Is there intelligent life on other planets?

at the sub-committee
investigating the Milky Way
scientists reported:

"We observed a
yellow dwarf star, type G2V,
its third planet.

spectrographic analysis shows an atmosphere comprising
78% nitrogen
20% oxygen
2% tear gas

mathematical models of its behaviour
indicate a core of iron
& surface crust of lead
flying sharply in all directions.

on one continent
polarised light detects
electric fields, formations of barbed wire.

radar mapping shows numerous craters
& laser beam reflections reveal sound waves
of sirens, screams, & weeping.

we conclude this evidence
irrefutably proves
that planet must have
intelligent life."

South African Radio Astronomy Observatory (photo https://www.sarao.ac.za)

Square Kilometre Array

Bernie Fanaroff 1947–
Justin Jonas 1958–

Sixty-four pylons hold up sixty-four ears
stitched together with threads of light
listening to the far side of our Milky Way:
all blinking in synch for correlator computers
huddled inside their Faraday cage

listening to the edgeless edges
of a universe with no centre;
expanding waves washing over stars
in the swirling arms of galaxies

listening to whispers from a pulsating vacuum
quantums of oscillating energy;
murmurs of dark matter

listening to ions
twirling in magnetic fields

listening in on the unknown

INDEX OF FIRST LINES

a standing ovation	10
as the sun sets	15
between moon & earth	69
bluest of planets	90
canals? faces? pyramids?	86
Classrooms produce martyrs	56
Commander Anatoli Solovyev	61
could Ed & the three-body problem	11
ESA commanded: create twins who shall seek	78
for one brief moment	68
full moon through silk of cloud	9
Give the museum your hourglass.	10
hamm-mmer	23
Heisenberg felt uncertain.	17
here, no angels sing	47
here, on every overhang & slippery stone	40
his maths kept coming out wrong – it was simplest to argue:	3
Houston, the eagle has landed	33
how? / how? / how?	35
"I believe that this nation should commit itself	75
ideas have ancestors	66
if you are a saint	26
If you land on Venus	82
in 1925 people were locked up as lunatic	10
in the garden of the late rocket designer	49
in the Indian River, even the fish try to fly	32
in the year that Holst composed *The Planets*	91
Isaac Newton never promised it would be easy	59
It is very difficult for me to write this letter, but I have	60
it's hard to live up to being a legend	5
Korolev commanded:	31
let this crew	67
lotsa crooners consume da moon 'n stars	89
Megawatt Park denies we have a power failure.	18
Mercury, fleetest of planets	81
Moon circles earth every 28 days	62

not just stormy, but størmier: Carl & Kristian   12

On a sun-singed steppe, Sergei stood, said: 30
On Andromeda Galaxy   93
on my first night   72
one moonful night   2

perched on mountainside shore of the great ocean   33
Pharaoh Nekau's explorers fantasised, argues Herodotus: 84

Remember silos of sentinels?   34
rings upon rings   88
seismologist selenologists   73
Sergei –   30
Sixty-four pylons hold up sixty-four ears   95
Syr Dar'ya   45

"Thank you for your patience.   92
that's one real good vibe   80
the Great Ocean   28
The Ministry for Exciting Machines decreed –   31
THE / MOON / IS / RISING   70
the visionary with a slide-rule named you: Silbervogel   42
there is no such thing as a boring Galilean satellite   87
these are the laws of physics   50
this aluminium aspires to heaven   22
this lance of fire   52
through a missing slat in the blind   74
today, your aunt's farm is a golf course   24
traditionalists always fear women who fly   57
tre / "if we imagine" argued Newton   43
Turbines roar, their rush surges through us   44
two hundred years ago   64

waiting for the civilised   83
we present our machine shop   76
we who are not angels   37
Wernher & Sergei dream with a slide-rule   27
When, in 1923, you published *Die Rakete zu den Planetenräumen* 25
when the stars fled Cape Town   14
when the sun sets   16
when Weimar dreamers got Third Reich budgets   33
when your salary isn't paid   7

you had to work your way through college   8
your birth   36

ACKNOWLEDGEMENTS

Some of these poems have been published in magazines, collections, websites, and anthologies: *www.Astronautix.com*, *www.badilishapoetry. com*, *Cape Times*, *Carapace*, *Contrast*, *Emergency Poems*, *English Academy Review*, *Focus English FAL LB Grade 11 Pearson*, *Heart of Africa*, *Illuminations*, *Imagination in a Troubled Space: A South African Reader*, *Jewish Affairs*, *Jewish Report*, *Kultur sprache Macht: Festschrift für Peter Horn*, *Mail & Guardian*, *New Coin*, *New Contrast*, *Oakland Journal*, *South African Institute of Physics 40th Annual Conference Programme*, *Under Lansdowne Bridge* and *Upstream*. Public readings include *Focal* and *Off the Wall*, and the 2001 Scifest.

The poem dedicated to Ed Belbruno, in the cycle "The Navigators" was set to music and sung by Elaine Walker at www.ziaspace.com (2000). It is included in the prize-winning documentary film by Jacob Okada, Carylanna Taylor, and Adam Morrow at www.paintingthewaytothemoon.com (2015).

The Chinese translation of "The Celestial Empire" is by Szu-chi Chen. The Hebrew translation of "A Star of David fell from Heaven" is by Devis Iosifzon.

www.ingramcontent.com/pod-product-compliance
Lightning Source LLC
Chambersburg PA
CBHW050817090426
42736CB00022B/3480